HAL•LEONARD

DRUM

PLAY·ALONG

blink-182

VOL. 10

Cover photo by Justin Stephens

Tracking, mixing, and mastering
by Jake Johnson & Bill Maynard at Paradyme Productions
Drums by Scott Schroedl
Guitars by Doug Boduch
Bass by Tom McGirr
Keyboards by Warren Wiegratz

ISBN 978-1-4234-1598-5

In Australia Contact:
Hal Leonard Australia Pty. Ltd.
4 Lentara Court
Cheltenham, Victoria, 3192 Australia
Email: ausadmin@halleonard.com.au

Visit Hal Leonard Online at www.halleonard.com

HAL•LEONARD®
CORPORATION
7777 W. BLUEMOUND RD. P.O. BOX 13819
MILWAUKEE, WISCONSIN 53213

HAL•LEONARD DRUM PLAY·ALONG

blink-182-

VOL. 10

CONTENTS

Adam's Song

Words and Music by Tom De Longe and Mark Hoppus

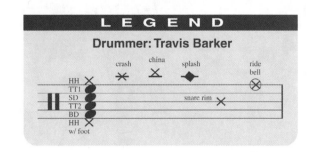

Intro
Moderate Rock ♩ = 136

We could-n't wait to get out - side. The world was wide,

too late to try. The tour was o - ver, we'd sur - vived.

To Coda

I could-n't wait till I got home to pass the time

Interlude

in my room a - lone.

D.S. al Coda

Coda

Interlude

in my room a - lone.

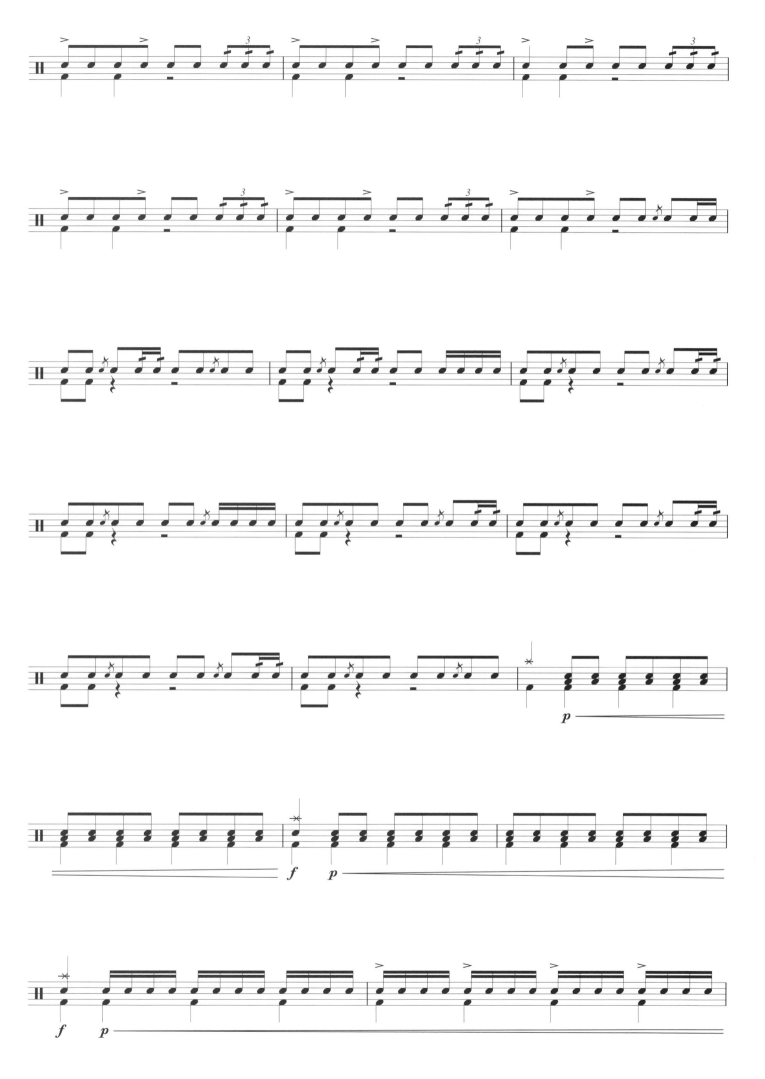

Chorus

I nev - er con - quered, rare - ly came.____ (But) to - mor - row

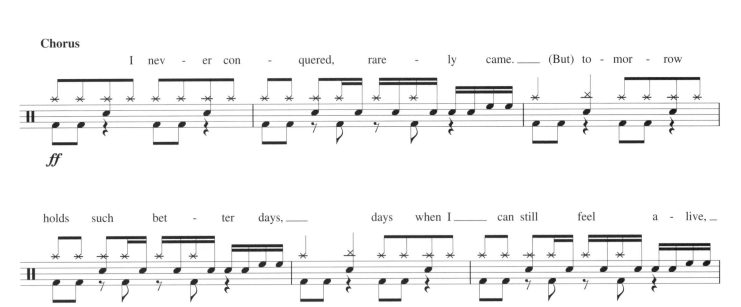

holds such bet - ter days,____ days when I ____ can still feel a - live,__

____ when I can't wait to get ____ out - side. The world __ is wide,__

____ the time ____ goes by. ____ The tour is o - ver, I've sur - vived.

I can't wait till I get home to pass the time_

____ in my room a - lone. ____

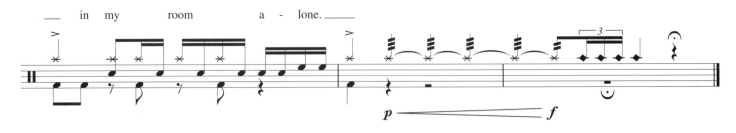

All the Small Things

Words and Music by Tom De Longe and Mark Hoppus

Coda

Na, na, na, na, na, na,_____ na, na, na, na. Na, na, na, na, na, na,_

Interlude

___ na, na, na, na.

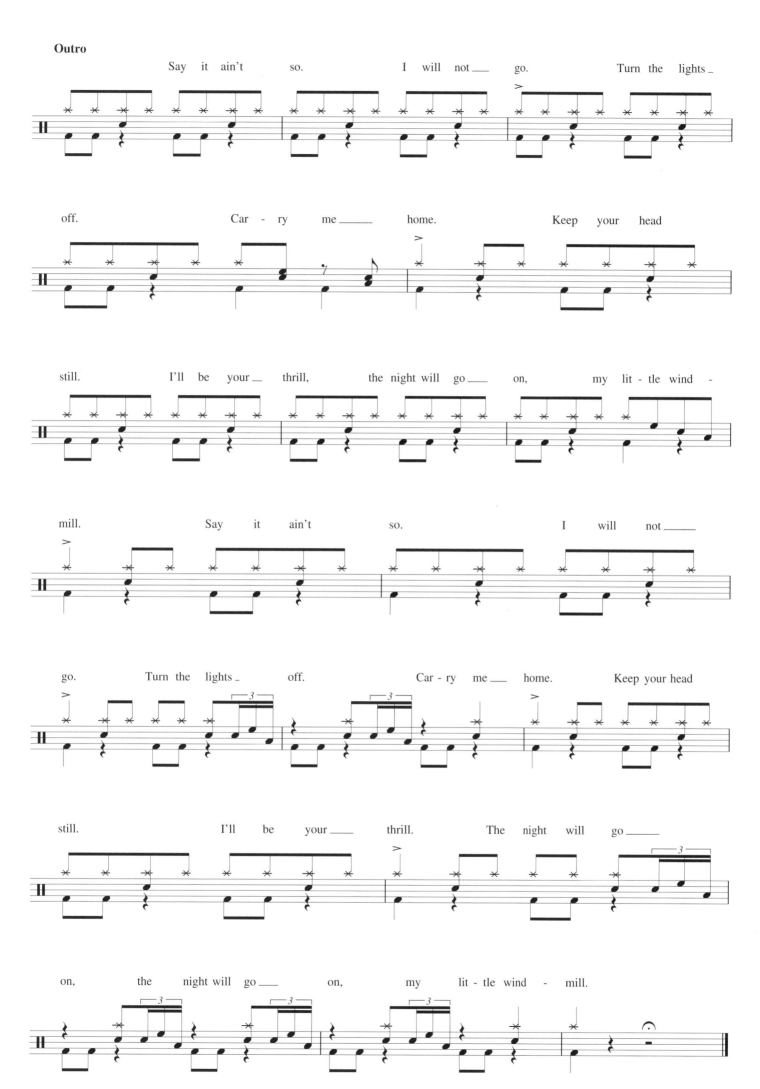

Dammit

Words and Music by Scott Raynor, Mark Hoppus and Tom De Longe

Intro
Fast Rock ♩ = 215

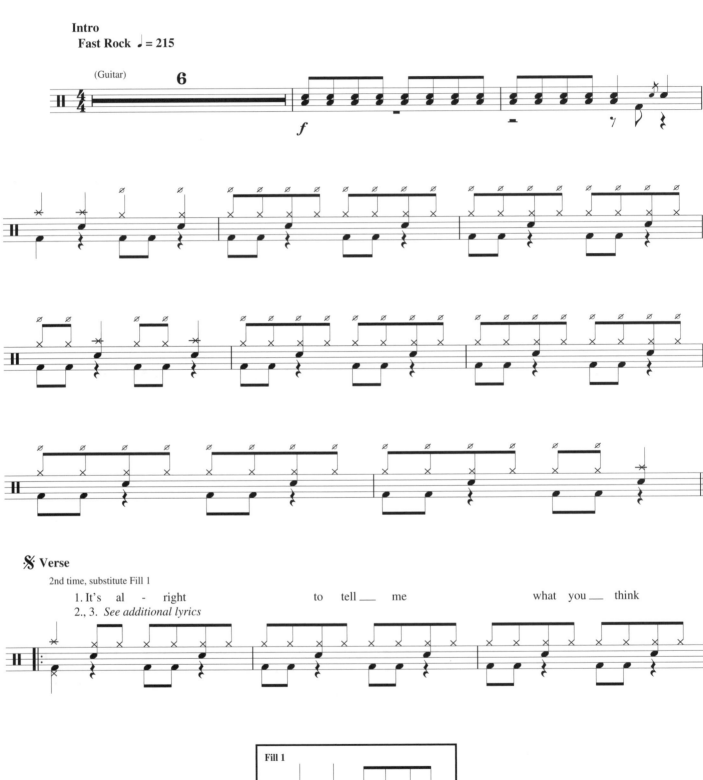

(Guitar)

𝄋 Verse

2nd time, substitute Fill 1

1. It's al - right   to tell ___ me   what you ___ think
2., 3. *See additional lyrics*

Fill 1

2.

Chorus
Half-time feel

now.　　　　　And it's hap-pened　　once　　a　-　gain,　　　　I'll

End half-time feel

turn　　　　to　a　　friend.　　　Some - one　　that　un - der -

Half-time feel

stands,　　　　sees　through　the　mas　-　ter　　plan.　　　　But

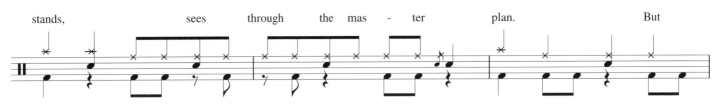

ev - 'ry - bod - y's　　　gone,　　　and I've　been here　for ___ too ___

End half-time feel

long　　　　　to　face this　　on ___ my ___　own.　Well, I　guess

this　is　　grow - ing　up.

Well, I   guess   this   is   grow - ing   up.

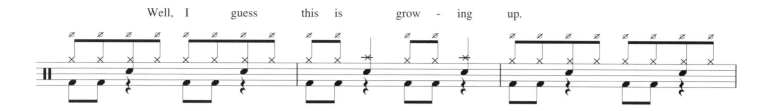

D.S. al Coda

⊕ Coda

Chorus
Half-time feel

back.   And   it - 'll   hap - pen   once ___ a -

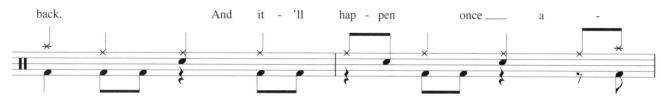

gain,   you'll   turn   to   a   friend.   Some -

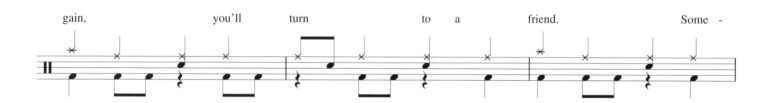

End half-time feel

one   that   un - der -   stands   and   sees   through   the   mas - ter

Half-time feel

plan.   But   ev - 'ry - bod - y's   gone,   and you've

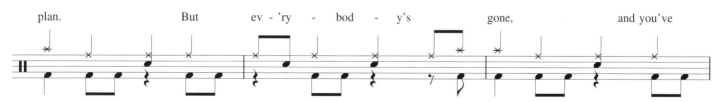

End half-time feel

been there   for ___ too ___ long   to   face   this   on ___ your ___

own.   Well,   I   guess   this   is   grow - ing

Interlude

up.

Well,   I   guess

Outro

this   is   grow - ing   up.

18

Well, I guess this is grow-ing up.

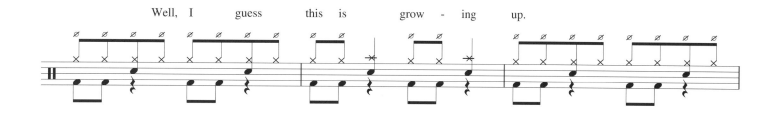

Well, I guess this is grow-ing

up.   Well, I guess

this is grow - ing up.

Well, I guess this is grow - ing up.

Additional Lyrics

2. The steps that I retrace, the sad look on your face.
   The timing and structure. Did you hear? He fucked her.
   A day late, a buck short. I'm writing the report
   On losing and failing. When I move I'm flailing now.

3. And maybe I'll see you at a movie sneak preview.
   You'll show up and walk by on the arm of that guy.
   And I'll smile and you'll wave, we'll pretend it's okay.
   The charade, it won't last. When he's gone and won't come back.

Feeling This

Words and Music by Travis Barker, Tom De Longe and Mark Hoppus

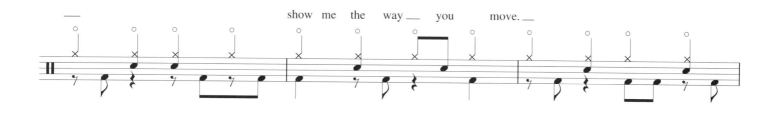

show me the way ___ you move. ___

Fuck it, it's such ___ a blur. ___ I love all the things ___ you do. ___

Chorus
Half-time feel

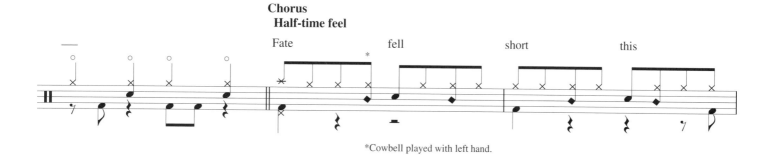

Fate fell short this

*Cowbell played with left hand.

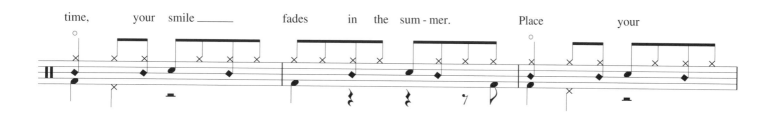

time, your smile _____ fades in the sum - mer. Place your

End half-time feel

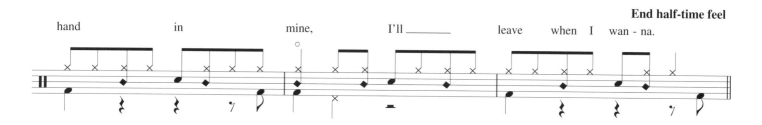

hand in mine, I'll _____ leave when I wan - na.

Interlude

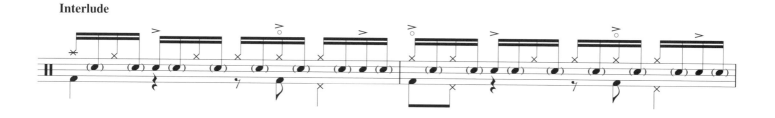

Verse

2. Where do we go __ from here? __   Turn all the lights __ down now. __

Smil - ing from ear __ to ear, __   our breath-ing has got __ too loud. __

__   Show me the bed - room floor, __

show me the bath - room mir - ror.   We're tak - ing this way __ too slow, __

__   take me a - way __ from here.

Chorus

Fate fell short this time, your smile _____

fades in the sum - mer. Place your hand in

22

Man Overboard

Words and Music by Tom De Longe and Mark Hoppus

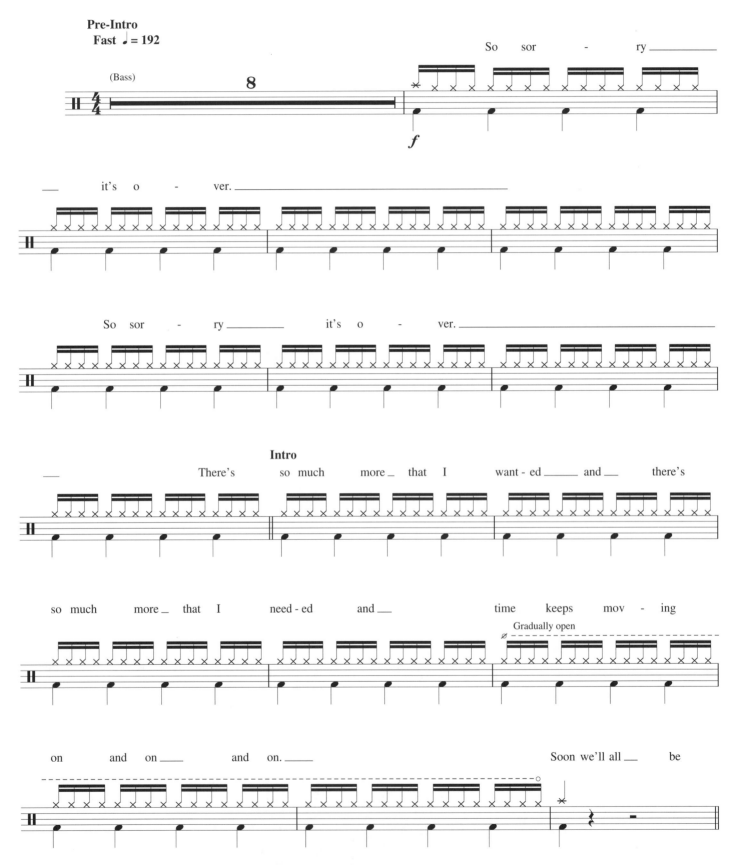

Interlude

gone.

Verse

1. Let's take some time _____ to talk this o - ver. _____

___ You're out of line _____ and real - ly so - ber. _____ We can't de - pend

There's so much more ___ that I want-ed and ___ there's so much more ___ that I need-ed and ___ time keeps mov-ing on and on ___ and on. ___

Soon we'll all ___ be gone. ___

Interlude

Outro

The Rock Show

Words and Music by Tom De Longe, Mark Hoppus and Travis Barker

Ev - 'ry - thing's   bet - ter when   she's   a - round.   I   can't wait 'til her par - ents go

To Coda 1 ⊕
To Coda 2 ⊕

out   of   town.   I   fell   in   love   with   the   girl   at   the rock   show.

Interlude

Verse

3. When we said   we were gon - na move to Veg - as,   I re - mem - ber the

look   her moth - er gave   us.   Sev - en - teen with - out a

D.S. al Coda 1

pur - pose or di - rec - tion.   We don't owe an - y - one a fuck - in' ex - pla - na - tion.

Coda 1

Bridge

Black and white pic - ture of her on my wall.   I   wait - ed

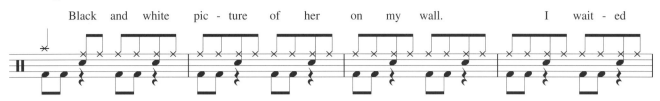

for her call.   She al - ways kept me wait - ing.

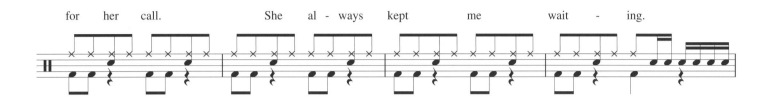

And if I ev - er got an - oth - er chance,   I'd still ask

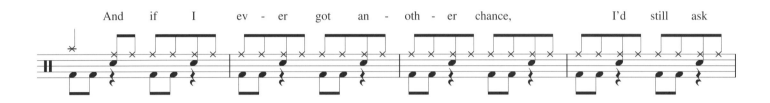

D.S. al Coda 2

her to dance   be - cause she kept me wait - ing. I

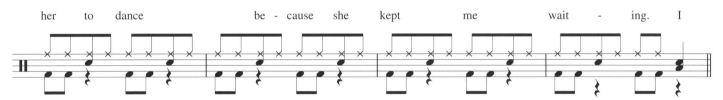

Coda 2

Outro

With the girl   at the rock show.

(I'll   nev - er   for -

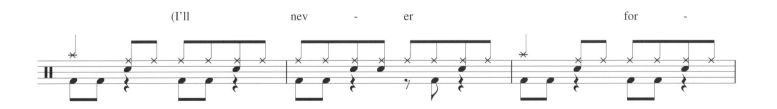

get to - night, I'll nev - er   for -

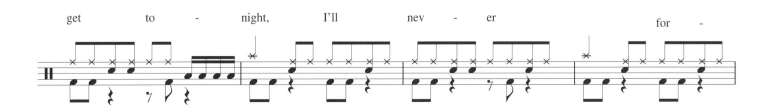

get   to   -   night,   I'll   nev   -   er

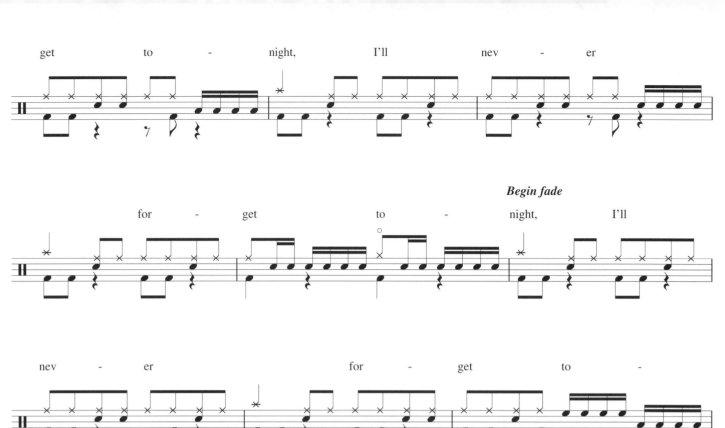

Begin fade

for   -   get   to   -   night,   I'll

nev   -   er   for   -   get   to   -

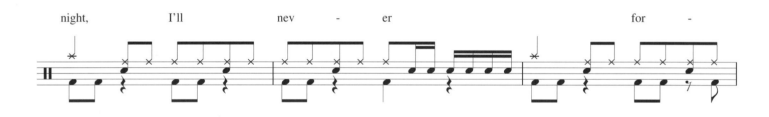

night,   I'll   nev   -   er   for   -

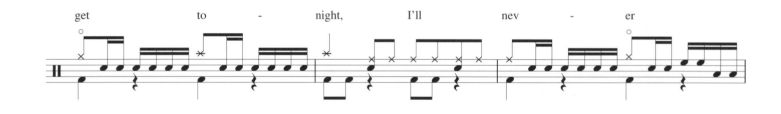

get   to   -   night,   I'll   nev   -   er

Fade out

nev   -   er   for   -   get   to   -

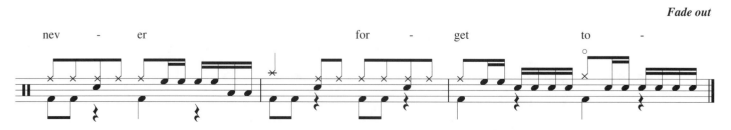

Stay Together
for the Kids

Words and Music by Tom De Longe, Mark Hoppus and Travis Barker

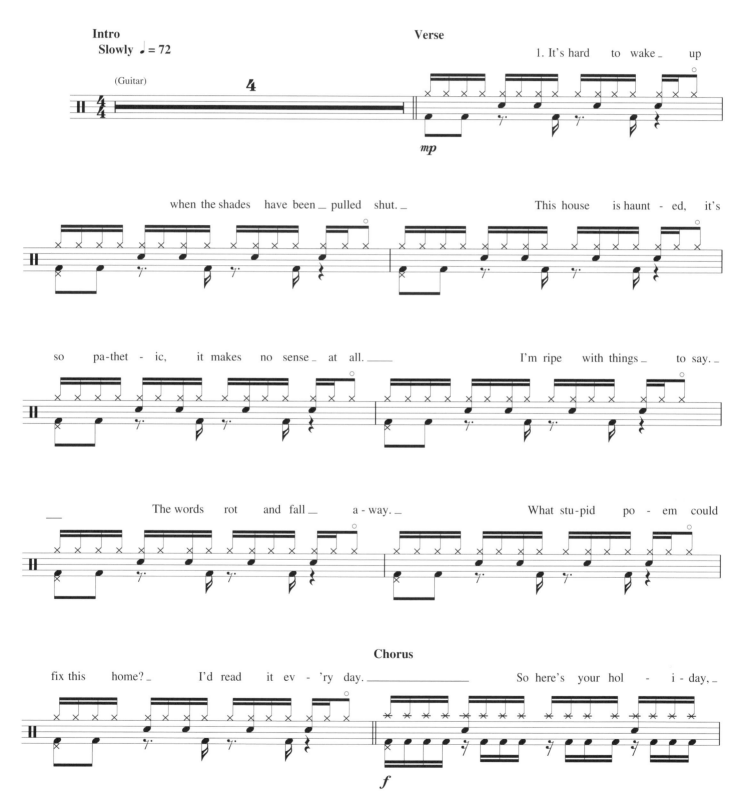

hope you en - joy it this time. You gave it all ___ a - way, ___

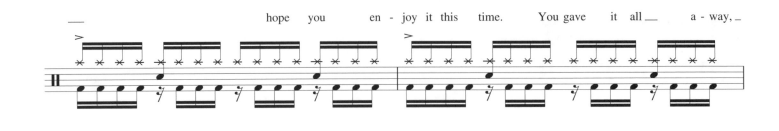

it was mine. _____ So when you're dead ___ and gone, ___

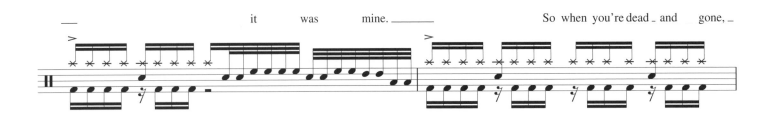

will you re - mem-ber this night? Twen - ty years ___ now lost, ___

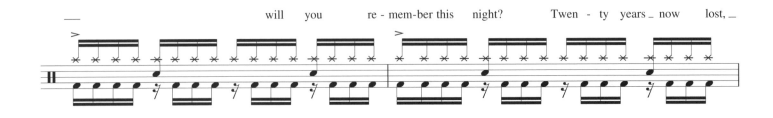

Interlude

it's not right.

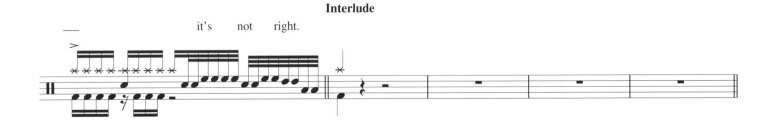

Verse

2. Their an - ger hurts ___ my ears, ___ been run-nin' strong for sev - en years. ___

mp

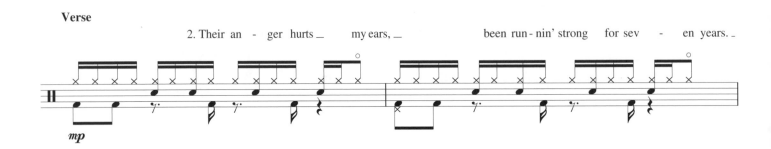

Rath-er than fix the prob - lems they nev - er solve ___ them. It makes no sense ___ at all. ___

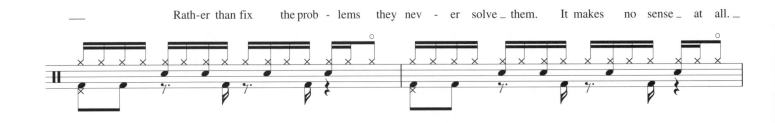

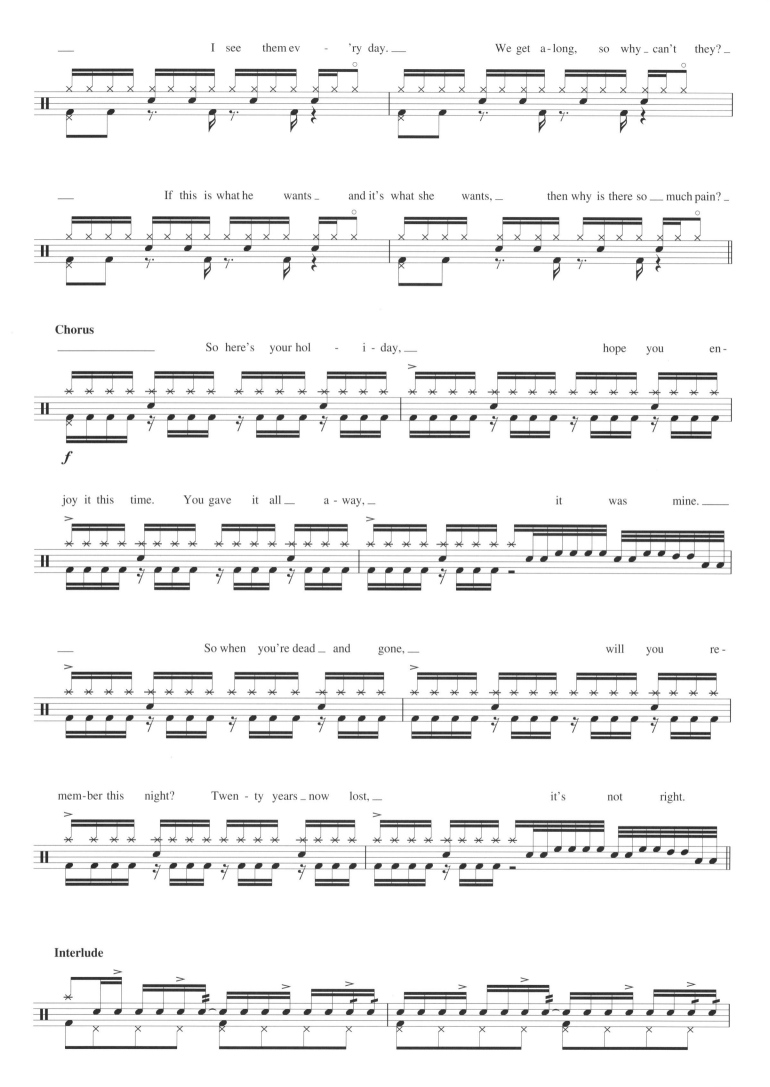

Chorus

Interlude

Chorus

So here's your hol - i - day, ___ hope you en-

joy it this time. You gave it all ___ a - way, ___ it was mine. ___

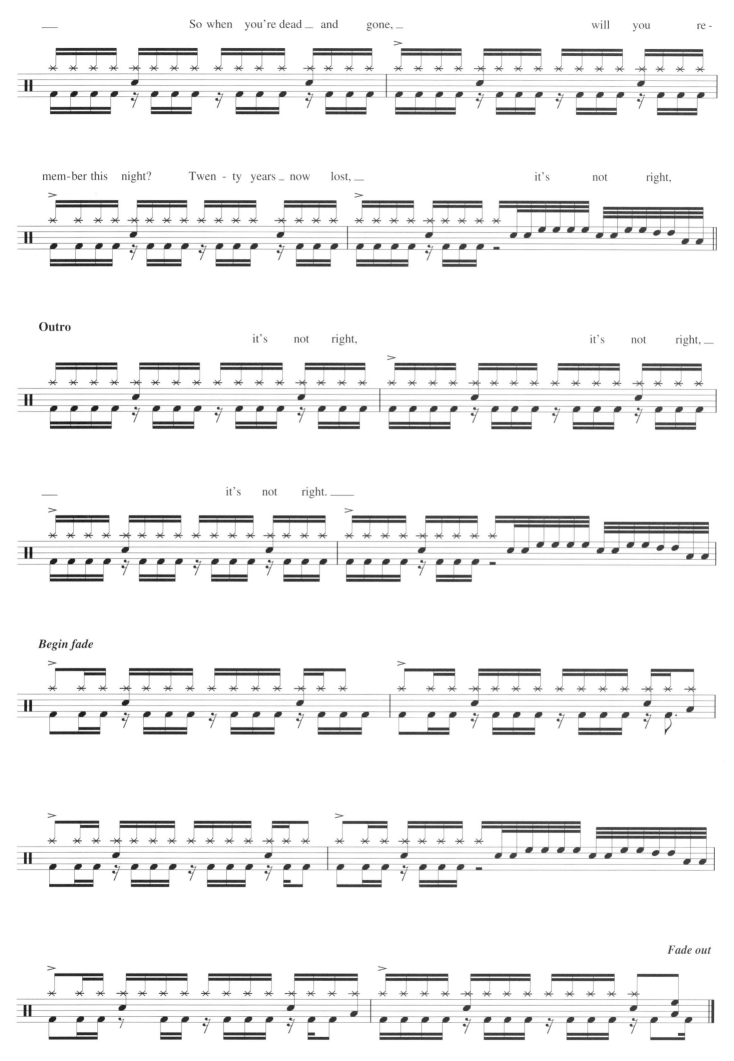

Outro

Begin fade

Fade out

What's My Age Again?

Words and Music by Tom De Longe and Mark Hoppus

twen - ty - three and are still more a - mused by prank phone calls.

What the hell is call I - D? My friends say I should act my age. What's my age a - gain?

Interlude

What's my age a - gain?

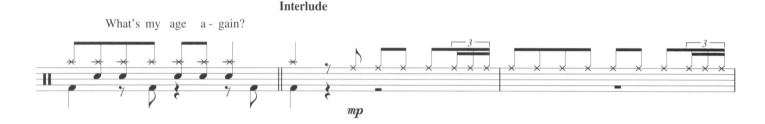

mp

D.S. al Coda

And that's a - bout the time she walked a -

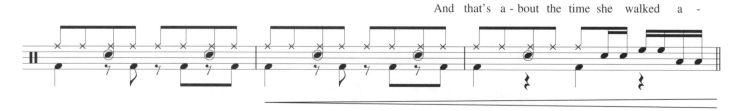

Coda

What's my age a - gain? That's a - bout the time that she broke

Chorus

up with me. No one should take them - selves so se - ri - ous - ly.

With man - y years a - head to fall in line, why should you wish that on me? I

nev - er wan - na act my age. What's my age a - gain? What's my age a - gain?

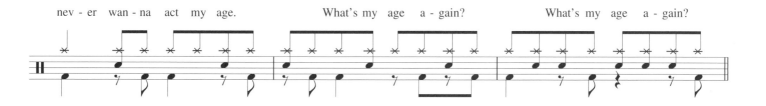

Outro

What's my age a - gain? _____

HAL•LEONARD DRUM PLAY•ALONG

Play your favorite songs quickly and easily with the *Drum Play-Along*™ series. Just follow the drum notation, listen to the CD to hear how the drums should sound, then play along using the separate backing tracks. The lyrics are also included for quick reference. The audio CD is playable on any CD player. For PC and Mac computer users, the CD is enhanced so you can adjust the recording to any tempo without changing the pitch!

Book/CD Packs

VOLUME 1 – POP/ROCK
Hurts So Good • Message in a Bottle • No Reply at All • Owner of a Lonely Heart • Peg • Rosanna • Separate Ways (Worlds Apart) • Swingtown.
00699742 Book/CD Pack $12.95

VOLUME 2 – CLASSIC ROCK
Barracuda • Come Together • Mississippi Queen • Radar Love • Space Truckin' • Walk This Way • White Room • Won't Get Fooled Again.
00699741 Book/CD Pack $12.95

VOLUME 3 – HARD ROCK
Bark at the Moon • Detroit Rock City • Living After Midnight • Panama • Rock You like a Hurricane • Run to the Hills • Smoke on the Water • War Pigs (Interpolating Luke's Wall).
00699743 Book/CD Pack $12.95

VOLUME 4 – MODERN ROCK
Chop Suey! • Duality • Here to Stay • Judith • Nice to Know You • Nookie • One Step Closer • Whatever.
00699744 Book/CD Pack $12.95

VOLUME 5 – FUNK
Cissy Strut • Cold Sweat, Part 1 • Fight the Power, Part 1 • Flashlight • Pick Up the Pieces • Shining Star • Soul Vaccination • Superstition.
00699745 Book/CD Pack $12.95

Prices, contents and availability subject to change without notice and may vary outside the US.

FOR MORE INFORMATION, SEE YOUR LOCAL MUSIC DEALER, OR WRITE TO:

HAL•LEONARD®
CORPORATION
7777 W. BLUEMOUND RD. P.O. BOX 13819 MILWAUKEE, WI 53213

Visit Hal Leonard Online at
www.halleonard.com

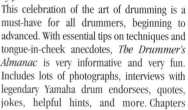

Drum Publications from
Peter Magadini

An internationally acclaimed performer, educator, and author, Peter Magadini has played with artists including Diana Ross, Mose Allison, George Duke, Chet Baker, Sonny Stitt, and more. He has also played percussion with The Berkshire Music Festival Orchestra at Tanglewood, The Toronto Symphony and The Fromm Festival of Contemporary Music at Carnegie Hall. In addition, Peter has performed as a studio musician in the US and Canada and has been featured on many recordings and with his own Quintet. Mr. Magadini holds percussion degrees from the University of Toronto and the San Francisco Conservatory of Music and includes among his teachers Donald Bothwell, Roland Kohloff, Roy Burns and North Indian Tabla Master Mahapurush Misra. Many of Peter's own students have received national and international recognition for their work.

THE COMPLETE DRUMSET RUDIMENTS
by Peter Magadini

Use your imagination to incorporate these rudimental etudes into new patterns that you can apply to the drumset or tom toms as you develop your hand technique with the *Snare Drum Rudiments*, your hand and foot technique with the *Drumset Rudiments* and your polyrhythmic technique with the *Polyrhythm Rudiments*. Adopt them all into your own creative expressions based on ideas you come up with while practicing. The recording includes demonstrations of the rudiments and four drum solos utilizing all of the rudiments.

_____ 06620016 Book/CD Pack $14.95

DRUMMER'S GUIDE TO MUSIC THEORY
by Peter Magadini

This is a complete guide to drum musicianship through the ears of a drummer. Topics include phrasing, chords, key signatures, the keyboard, the guitar, ear training, scales, and how to listen while playing.

_____ 00849165 ....$7.95

LEARN TO PLAY THE DRUMSET
by Peter Magadini

This method has been written to teach the basics of the drum set in the shortest amount of time. The method is unique in that it is a beginning course that starts the student out on the entire drum set. Book One covers basic set-ups, reading and improvisation, coordination of hands and feet, and features a variety of contemporary and basic rhythm patterns with exercise breakdowns for each. Book Two continues instruction with more improvisation exercises, playing triplets, flams and flam beats, practical musicianship tips, equipment selection and many more techniques and skills. The CD features demonstrations of exercises.

_____ 06620030 Book 1/CD Pack $14.95
_____ 06620031 Book 2/CD Pack $14.95
_____ 06620000 Book 1 Only...$7.95
_____ 06620001 Book 2 Only...$5.95

LEARN TO PLAY THE DRUMSET DVD VHS
by Peter Magadini

The perfect way to start a beginner on the entire drumset! This informative and descriptive DVD: takes you through the basics of four- and five-piece drum set-ups (and how to tune them); illustrates the grips and how to use the sticks; teaches the staff, time values, double strokes and counting; and much more. Using patterns drawn from a wide variety of musical styles, you'll learn how to play a drum fill, an open roll, a closed roll, flams, paradiddles, and single- and double-stroke combinations as they apply to the drumset. Includes an 8-page booklet with diagrams and other useful information. Use the DVD or video by itself or with Peter Magadini's *Learn to Play the Drumset, Book 1.* 44 minutes.

_____ 00320382 DVD $19.95
_____ 06621754 VHS Video $19.95

POLYRHYTHMS – THE MUSICIAN'S GUIDE
by Peter Magadini
edited by Wanda Sykes

Peter Magadini's *Polyrhythms* is acclaimed the world over and has been hailed by *Modern Drummer* magazine as "by far the best book on the subject." Written for instrumentalists and vocalists alike, this book/CD pack contains excellent solos and exercises that feature polyrhythmic concepts. Topics covered include: 6 over 4, 5 over 4, 7 over 4, 3 over 4, 11 over 4, and other rhythmic ratios; combining various polyrhythms; polyrhythmic time signatures; and much more. The CD includes demos of the exercises.

_____ 06620053 Book/CD Pack $19.95

FOR MORE INFORMATION, SEE YOUR LOCAL MUSIC DEALER, OR WRITE TO:

HAL•LEONARD® CORPORATION
7777 W. BLUEMOUND RD. P.O. BOX 13819 MILWAUKEE, WI 53213

Visit Hal Leonard Online at **www.halleonard.com**
Prices, contents and availability subject to change without notice.

0707